THE
QUEST
— FOR —
PEACE

Quelling the Rash of Violence

Harry Gael Michaels

20 Twenty
Literary Group

The Quest for Peace: Quelling the Rash of Violence
Copyright © 2023 by Harry Gael Michaels

ISBN
978-1-961250-74-1 (Paperback)
978-1-961250-75-8 (eBook)
978-1-962868-18-1 (Hardcover)

The Quest for Peace

Table of Contents

Dedication

This book is dedicated to all the young innocent children and their teachers who have been senselessly slaughtered in their own classrooms by the violent and hateful dispositions of those who are reflecting the malcontent in our society as a whole.

Foreword

If there is light in the soul,
There will be beauty in the person,

If there is beauty in the person,
There will be harmony in the house.

If there is harmony in the house,
There will be order in the nation.

If there is order in the nation,
There will be peace in the world.

Chinese Proverb

Life is absurd and beautiful. When you consider that life, as we know it, has a beginning, a flourishing, a decline and an end. We wonder why we constantly endeavor to race forward in the never-ending struggle for ascendancy and advancement? For what? As William Shakespeare put it in his Act 2, Scene 7 of his play, As You Like It:

JAQUES

All the world's a stage,
And all the men and women merely players:
They have their exits and their entrances;
And one man in his time plays many parts,
His acts being seven ages. At first the infant,
Mewling and puking in the nurse's arms.
And then the whining school-boy, with his satchel
And shining morning face, creeping like snail
Unwillingly to school. And then the lover,
Sighing like furnace, with a woeful ballad
Made to his mistress's eyebrow. Then a soldier,
Full of strange oaths and bearded like the pard,
Jealous in honor, sudden and quick in quarrel,
Seeking the bubble reputation
Even in the cannon's mouth. And then the justice,
In fair round belly with good capon lined,
With eyes severe and beard of formal cut,
Full of wise saws and modern instances;
And so, he plays his part. The sixth age shifts
Into the lean and slipper's pantaloon,
With spectacles on nose and pouch on side,
His youthful hose, well saved, a world too wide
For his shrunk shank; and his big manly voice,
Turning again toward childish treble, pipes
And whistles in his sound. Last scene of all,
That ends this strange eventful history,
Is second childishness and mere oblivion,
Sans teeth, sans eyes, sans taste, sans everything.

So, what drives us toward endless toil and production? As our shrinking energy steals, inch by inch, our vitality and stamina. And, hoping that something after death from whose bourn no traveler returns, will satisfy all our longings, return all our losses and gratify all our desires.

And, then there is; "The Man with the Hoe," the poem
by Ewin Markham that begins with:
Bowed by the weight of centuries he leans,
Upon his hoe and gazes at the ground,
The emptiness of ages in his face,
And on his back the burden of the world.
Who made him dead to rapture and despair,
A thing that grieves not and that never hopes,
Stolid and stunned, a brother to the ox?
Who loosened and let down this brutal jaw?
Whose was the hand that slanted back this brow?
Whose breath blew out the light within this brain?

Is this the Thing the Lord God made and gave?
To have dominion over sea and land;
To trace the stars and search the heavens for power;
To feel the passion of Eternity.

And yet, stop and consider all that homo sapiens has accomplished, created and produced throughout its short time on this earth. That is the beauty of life, from ancient tools made of stone, to the discovery of fire, the wheel, metal weapons, agriculture, animal husbandry, the steam engine and the industrial revolution, the architecture and engineering of great cathedrals and pyramids; astrological discoveries, science, medicine and aviation, the Apollo

II moon-shot, digital technology, the arresting of many fatal diseases that formerly wiped out huge populations, cell phones, computers and now plans to go to Mars. However, there is also the Achilles' heel of our nature, and that is the phenomenon of endless unrest and disquietude in the quest for peace because it seems so elusive whether it be within ourselves or within our societies. This essay is about that quest.

Prologue

Religion has sought to show us the way, by giving us the most powerful and elemental motivators, in the form of reward (heaven) or punishment (hell). But since we have acquired more knowledge and awareness of our condition in this life, are the fundamental religions enough to set us free to feel the passion of eternity?

The king of Bhutan in north eastern India thought that the wellbeing and peace of the people is so important that he declared in 1972, "The nation should value its Gross National Happiness before its Gross National Product." The King, Jigme Singye Wangchuck, did not talk of heaven and hell, but he talked of good democratic government, good health, good education and preserving the best of their culture and environment. Happiness is a concern about endorsing and maintaining good ethics, morality and peace. We know that Bhutan is a far cry from the USA in every way, however, we might learn something of their culture that could serve us well, as we move forward into the 21st century with all its stresses and complications.

Daily in the news, we hear of disturbing events of violence, disorder and dissatisfaction within our society and with our political leaders. The Democrats tell us that our president is fostering a schism of racial, social, economic and political discontent while the Republicans are trying to maintain a bulwark against total collapse of our democratic institutions. Even though the tax law was readjusted to be more equitable, we are paying more taxes. The cost of medical care and vital medications keep going up while the quality of medical services keep going down, even as doctors feel more pressure to conform to bureaucratic and legal constraints.

Children in school can no longer feel safe in their classrooms and parents must spend hours driving their kids to and from school for fear that some lunatic running loose in their neighborhood will abduct their child. Since Columbine, 20 years ago, there has been a din of frantic conversation about what to do about guns and disturbed individuals having access to them, as the heart-breaking news of young children and teachers being massacred in their own classrooms, becomes more frequent. Rapid fire automatic firearms, with high capacity magazines, which were designed for military use in combat, are accessible to the pathologically unstable.

"When and how is all this disorder going to be brought to an end?" we asked. Why are our political leaders so lacking in courage to take the necessary steps to do the things that are needed to bring the Ship of State back on a steady course? Where is the spirit of collegiality that was once the hallmark of our Congress?

"No matter how noble the objectives of a government, if it blurs decency and kindness, cheapens human life and breeds ill-will and suspicion. It is an evil government."

—Eric Hoffer

I started my career, back in the'60s, as a juvenile probation officer, when offensive behavior on the part of juveniles amounted to petty theft, vandalism, joy riding, misbehavior at home or at school, and an occasional breaking and entering; but very little violence and certainly nothing like it is today. Very often, these kinds of events could be handled by the probation officer in conjunction with parental cooperation and school personnel, with a low recidivism rate of about 15%. Our economy supported most parents in the supervision of their small children by enabling a working man to adequately support his family while the mother stayed at home. Educational personnel were highly respected as professional and caring mentors. People had a feeling for their communities and neighborhoods and our political leaders seemed invested in the overall welfare of the people of the United States as their primary responsibility. They might argue and banter back and forth about some proposed legislation but after words had been spoken and compromises made, they would go out and drink beer together in a spirit of camaraderie.

However, the'60s also marked the beginning of a great social upheaval in this country as the progeny of the WWII generation in confluence with the emergence of the black population under Martin Luther King, Jr. began to assert their legitimate influence as movers in the destiny of America. We had assassinations, presidential disgrace, Vietnam, and the threat of nuclear war with the Soviet Union. A great anxiety and pall seemed to settle over the US. When all this happened, those of a marginal and unbalanced character, erupted into a frenzy of drugs and violence, as a way of expressing their discontent and anomie. Mistrust and a consequent excessive litigation also filled the air, like smog. Our prisons and jails became glutted with the wreckage of humanity and little was done to salvage those unfortunate misfits of our society, as we continued to wage the "war on drugs." Homeless populations became rampant in our cities.

It was during this time that I went to grad school to study psychology and child development, because I became fascinated with the question, why do some people become at war with themselves or with others while others go in peace and contentment? I don't believe in the religious sentiment that some fall prey to the devil, therefore are lost, and either must be salvaged through evangelism or doomed to eternal perdition in hades. My essay is all about this question. What bends a personality, from childhood, toward good or evil? This is a perennial question that existed since the beginning of time. Religion relates a story of a rebellious Archangel, Lucifer who rebelled against God and became the devil; and the principal proprietor of hell who seeks to tempt God's people into his domain, along with the "sin" of Adam and Eve that stained the innocent souls of God's fallen children. I, rather, prefer to see what we call evil, as a distorted character development through faulty pedagogy and poor community support. That is what my essay is about. It looks more deeply into early childhood development and how the personality is molded.

The first part of my essay considers how religion has been used, historically, as a buttress against the existential anxiety of being in a threatening world of danger, disease, natural disasters and death. If one can imagine a God that can be beseeched, and who has the power to alleviate all these fears and concerns, then it helps cope with the ordinary tasks of living. However, if a possible eternal life of torment and misery is possible, it introduces a kind of thinking that produces an us-and-them perspective. That can be at the heart of a pedagogy that, as Carl Jung, the famous Swiss psychiatrist taught, is a denial of one's full nature, the acknowledgement of the shadow side. When we are taught to become one way instead of another, which may dampen our true inclination, we may feel we have to repress part of ourselves in order to receive approval and salvation from hell or avoid retaliation or abandonment. We can become estranged to part of ourselves and become only a partial being, ravaged by doubt and loneliness. If one develops a character of doubt and loneliness, that person may develop injurious aberrant compensations toward himself or toward others. The Robert Louis Stevenson story of "Dr Jekyll and Mr. Hyde," is the symbolic story of a man and his shadow. The shadow refers to everything that has been repressed and embodies all of life that has not been allowed expression, and like the devil, needs to be acknowledged and mastered, or it will forever vie for ascendency. The more frightened and isolated one becomes, the more likely that individual will resort to an extreme reaction, such as shooting up children on a school ground.

These considerations lead into a discussion of the incidence of gun violence in America and some relevant statistics. There is some merit in looking at the origin of the 2nd amendment and why it was established in the first place? The terrible crimes, with guns, that have been perpetrated since Columbine (which opens in my book, How Goes it With America?), is a disgrace to our national character. The attacks on innocent children in school is unconscionable, and the lack of resolve among our legislators to effectively deal with the problem is inexcusable. Again, the essence of these writings is to look, more carefully and fundamentally, at the causes of such disorders. We cannot continue to just babble and fret endlessly while the public becomes inured, as in a frog that finds himself in a pot of gradually heating water, which he becomes adjusted to until he finds it so hot that he must jump out but is too weak to save himself. Violence in our society is a cancer in the organism, and unless we address it intelligently, it will destroy us. We are the most violent, developed country in the world with such a problem.

The next part of this essay deals with criminality and aberrant character development, and the origins of punishment as a means of controlling human behavior, and as a way of deferring to God and the leader of the tribe. Then, an historical summary of crime and punishment, beginning in the early Mesopotamian-era and on up through Western Civilization with the advent of Christianity's influence, and culminating in the most recent methods of adjudicating criminal behavior. We have a very high recidivism rate in the United States, which is a waste of human resources. So, we look at other better ways of dealing with the criminally disposed, taking Norway's penal system as an example of looking at reclaiming human resources.

The final part of this essay explores professional studies and ideas that have been developed, to address the problems of faulty child development, with special reference to the importance of family, the school and the community. The basic elements of motivation, as described by Abraham Maslow and his hierarchy of needs, explain how basic needs form the platform on which one can pass through the developmental tasks as described by Eric Ericson, and also how the thwarting of these needs can lead to a condition Maslow calls, the "psycho-pathogenesis of threat." There is also a discussion of brain function and how certain elements in the brain become conditioned to set the stage for a happy or sad disposition, and the kind of choices one makes to either enhance a positive or a negative self, a full life of affirmation or a diminished life of defeat, a life of peace or a life of war.

THE QUEST *for* PEACE

From whence in the world comes peace and gratification? Obviously, not from God nor from Christ nor from any of the sages down through the ages.

Peace in the world is something that God, through Jesus and others, has beckoned us to achieve. However, it is up to us to pursue and accomplish. But how?

Just as everything has developmental stages, such as the evolutionary steps of child development into adulthood, so it is with the evolutionary processes of the human condition:

- Step one is economic, with the necessities of life such as food, water, and protection from threats to one's existence.
- Step two is political, with the formation of tribes and communities for protection and survival, leaders and followers.
- Step three is sociological, with the aspiration to achieve status, prestige, and personal accomplishment within the group or community.
- Step four is psychological and spiritual, with a need to achieve self-fulfillment, full functioning as a person and spiritual edification. Science, Medicine, Technology, Arts and Education.

Individual human development and evolution starts with:

- Step one, which involves safety and security with food, water, and protection.
- Step two, which deals with belonging, personal relationships, family, friends and tribal associations
- Step three, which involves personal esteem, prestige, and accomplishment within a community.
- Step four, which deals with actualization, striving toward full potential and full functioning; creativity and productivity—Abraham Maslow.

Religion has always been indigenous to the human condition. It, nevertheless, can be an opiate if we artificially alleviate the existential anxiety of our lives, and keeps us from maturing into a more rational state of mind, if we don't temper those sentiments with the executive function of our brains. Having been raised as a Catholic myself and educated by the Jesuits up through college, I am aware of the dark elements of that religion that negatively affect self-direction and moral responsibility; as I continue to look for the light as well.

Because life, considered historically, has been so fraught with tribulation and threat, primitive man found that by using his imagination he could contrive elaborate projected personified powers, rituals and icons, that he could refer to in times of crises, to alleviate his fear and anxiety about survival and death. But this, by and large, is delusion and fantasy.

Religion, then, has been a bedrock function of making fundamental sense out of threatening perplexity. It has been an essential way of quelling the primitive brain, so that one could lead a life of some emotional security and sensibility. And because of the immediacy and functional necessity of religion, it became an exclusive rite of tribal coherence. Religion became so dominant in the history of sapiens that brutal wars and terrors had become mental constructs to protect tribal delusions, when tribes lived close to each other.

The evolution of sapiens is the evolution of rationality, temperance, and circumspection from delusional belief systems to reasonable faith in life and its destiny, which, by the way, does not discount the possibility of an afterlife as a faith because that kind of faith doesn't insult or offend one's rationality as something that defies our intelligence. One can always hope and wish and look for evidence of such a continued existence.

Religion has the quality for children that provides a wonder world of magical fascination, somewhat like the Santa Claus myth, while religion for adults provides an avenue for pursuing the mature teleological impulse for greater spirituality, wisdom and faith. Carl Jung, the famous creator of analytical psychology, said that "Religion is to be an activity for the mature, in the second half of life– not to be imposed on children with notions of a God that punishes with threats of hell if not obedient to the elders of the Church."

That, it seems to me, is a legitimate way of looking at religion; it doesn't defy our senses and sensibilities. It expresses hope and a deep desire, and a reaching for something better in our lives. The motivation for making life safer and more fulfilling, is what we see, in all we have accomplished throughout human history. The distressing part is how we have woven into our evolution such confusion, complexity and destruction by constructing dogmas, institutional-isms and Bible-thumping, and then forming impenetrable walls— to protect and defend against those who would be outside our walls of self-righteousness. The essence of religion, in my view, is the brotherhood of Man under the fatherhood of God.

The history of the Church, I was raised in, is a history of defensiveness against a perception of threat to its fragile, delusional integrity. I say delusional because most of Christian theology (but not all) about Jesus of Nazareth is a mythological construct supported only by references to questionable quotes (the Gospels) from Jesus, himself, decades after his death. By the way, there is no record of Jesus having written anything himself, as to what his intentions were.

To someone steeped in religious beliefs, it can be frightening to think that we, alone, are responsible for peace and the good in the world because Christian children are taught that it is sinful to assume personal responsibility for making one's own judgments regarding moral issues. Children are taught that they must always defer to the authority of the Church, under threat of losing their immortal soul, for their moral and spiritual judgments and guidance. On the other hand, however, it can also be re-assuring, if a child is taught and encouraged to understand that there is no devil, and the possibility of an eternity in damnation and suffering in the fires of hell, is only a fanatical and mythological construct designed to manage and control the flock of anxious believers. My faith is that our God, and I believe there is a supreme/ultimate cause of universal creation, we will be in consonance with universal design by taking up this challenge ourselves rather than relying on a childish prayerfulness in the hope of having Divine intervention do it for us. As the vice-minister of His Majesty's Air Service in England said during the great "Battle of Britain" in WWII, "If all we can do is get down on our knees and pray...God help us." "God helps those who help themselves" is a saying I heartily endorse as well, "Feed a man a fish and you feed him for a day. Teach him how to fish and you feed him for a lifetime." These thoughts foster self-reliance and responsibility rather than anxious dependence.

So, what must we, as a people of this mysterious and wonderful existence, make of all this? I say mysterious because when you stop to consider our earth so infinitesimally tiny within our vast galaxy of our universe (our galaxy being only one of indeterminant numbers) it seems mind boggling that we are either alone in this vast universe or we are not alone. Either way, it is indeed a humbling thought. Why us? It seems to me, is a valid question. Why are we here? We must move forward, as *Homo sapiens* have always done, toward some unknown destiny. The destiny is the movement, not the destination. Religion, however, helps us fulfil the need for an explainable destiny and does not defy the reason which we were endowed with by our Creator.

When I was in the second grade, at a Catholic parochial elementary school, the nuns taught with a catechism that answered this basic question by saying, "God made us to love, serve, honor and obey him in this world so we can be happy with Him in the next."

The only objection I have to this way of thinking is that it denies that we can be happy in this world. In my view, God would want us to be happy here in this world; serving, loving, and obeying our better angels or rationality in congruence with our lower emotional sensitivities rather than being at eternal war within ourselves, and with others; and fearing the possibility of spending an eternity in isolation from all that we have known to be good.

It is my contention that the road to peace lies not in trying to achieve sanctimonious religious perfection or masochistic martyrdom but in fully embracing the gift of life that God has given us as we find it.

Where does evil come from, as taught in Christian Sunday school, if it does not come from an Archangel named Lucifer who decided one day that he wanted to challenge God for His Majesty and usurp His power and position, and then to be cast out of paradise and charged with ruling over hell with a vengeful disposition of getting back at God by seducing His creatures away from Him and into the pit of everlasting torment. Quite a horror story. That's what Christians are taught as children. This takes evil out of our hands and places it where we can only fear falling into the beckoning of the ever-present devil always tempting to lure little children away from God. Why would an all loving, all knowing, all just, all omniscient God create people in the first place He knew beforehand, were destined to go to Hell. Free Will?

Free will cannot be attributed to innocent children since they have no free will and adults have varying degrees of this capacity.

We would probably all agree that evil is characterized by intent to lie, cheat, steal, destroy, exploit others, brutalize, and maim. Evil's antecedents are discontent, feelings of threat and rejection, dissatisfaction, deprivation and a state of war within our-selves, or war with others. We turn bad feelings, anger, and resentment into destructive action inward toward ourselves, or outward against others.

Gun Violence

To gun or not to gun
That is the question:
Whether'tis nobler in the mind to suffer the
slings and arrows of outrageous school atrocities
or to take arms against a sea of childhood terror and,
by opposing, end them.'Tis a resolution devoutly to
be wished.

The issue of gun control and school violence has become an epidemic in this country. We are the only advanced nation in the world with such threats to children in school. We ask, "What has happened in the United States to account for these events and what can be effectively done about it?"

Many agree that there is an insidious moral/ethical disease pervading our society, which appears to have begun with a desperate upheaval of social mores and racial discontent during the 1960s and the "Age of Aquarius."

Even the Catholic Church decided to "modernize," to accommodate many who were leaving the Church, for a relaxation of rigid dogmatic rules.

Then there was the Vietnam war which split the country and drove many young people to take up residence in Canada. History proved that entering this conflict was not only a colossal mistake, but it even destroyed and undermined the confidence and respect for our military leaders; and the misled GIs that offered their service with belief and trust in their country's leadership and good will. Next came the series of assassinations of John, and Robert Kennedy, and then Martin Luther King, Jr.

In 1974 President Nixon and Vice President Agnew were found guilty of serious crimes and could no longer hold honorable office. Later, in 1999, another President of the United States, William Clinton, was impeached for defaming the Presidency of the United States by perpetrating a salacious, sexual act in the Oval Office, and then committing perjury about it. Is it any wonder that the children of this country have lost faith in just what this country stands for, and its sacred values? With all the atrocities committed in the schools against children and their teachers, is it any wonder that there is great anxiety and instability in America. Children and adults, not to mention veterans, are committing suicide at an alarming rate, and many are resorting to drugs to alleviate their distress.

It is my contention that society must be a bulwark of support and stability, and when that bulwark begins to crumble, the most unstable will break down and resort to violence as the anxiety and depression become too intense for them to handle. Ethics and responsibility have broken down in business, industry, and politics. Today, one must struggle to find any truth in advertising since so much is an attempt to sell a product of questionable value.

There was a time when a product with the seal, "Made in the USA" was a symbol of pride of accomplishment, and fine workmanship in America. We have not seen that in some time. Our children are growing up confused, anxious, and depressed and, in addition, they now must be fearful of even the sanctuary of school because their elders are not of a will to courageously deal with the criminally disposed and mentally disturbed, who will get their hands on unregulated guns and murder innocent children, and their teachers…teachers, by the way, who are grossly lacking in sufficient monetary rewards and professional respect for their service.

Let's look for a minute at the second amendment gun issue that is so guardedly protected. This amendment to the constitution was adopted way back in the 18th century, when America was a new and struggling nation. Life was still quite primitive, and people lived on outlying farms and small communities and were subject to attack by outlaws, animals, Indians, and even British sympathizers. They recognized that they needed firearms for self-protection. There was very little law enforcement in those days. So, it made sense to have a rifle or two. Today, however, we live in a highly civilized society with extensive police protection, courts, and systems of law enforcement. It seems almost insane to think that we need unrestricted gun laws, as interpreted by the NRA, because of a fear and paranoia of encroachment by our own government. The second amendment was appropriate for early America, within the context of why it was established in the first place, but not for today. There is no need in our society for weapons that were designed for military combat. Rifles and handguns for those that want them, ought to be licensed and registered; much as we require for use of an automobile.

For the time being, there must be highly trained individuals (I would say two or three) in the use and possession of firearms, who are present in the schools, and can immediately confront any incursion with an intent to harm. There must be strict and sensible dress codes so that no one will feel intimidated by others or be able to conceal a weapon. Bullying and intimidation of a student must be totally zeroed out, and any violation must be dealt with harshly. There is no excuse or justification for bullying and intimidation. There ought to be group counselling for those who are so inclined, so no student would feel excluded or isolated among the student body.

Violence, I am persuaded, comes from a lack of affinity with one's society, so to speak, or feelings of social isolation. Man, it has been said many times, is a social animal. This has been demonstrated many times in the circumstances of small children. When children are isolated from human warmth and contact, they suffer a condition of emotional shutdown that is tantamount to death. Isolation can be perceived as a sense of alienation from oneself or from within the society or tribe. Highly associated with isolation are mistrust, anomie, nihilism and eventual despair. The outcome is often projected violence against others and oneself. Contented people are those that feel connected– in trust within themselves, and each other.

Many have wisely pointed out that this problem must be addressed at a time of early child development. Children must be raised in a secure, stable, and predictable environment with the three elements of family, school, and community. Family is the essential foundation that initiates and supports the child's developmental tasks, and the emergence of his/her character. Parents, therefore, must be capable of providing the warmth and attention that a child needs to grow strong and self-assured. The school is designed to reinforce this character development through education and acculturation, and finally, the community will be the workshop in which the emerging adult can practice what he/she has been taught and experienced.

There is much fine literature and professional instruction available today to all those concerned with raising healthy, happy and productive children and stemming the terrible epidemic of violence and mayhem that is all around us. We all must take a proactive stance against this cancerous growth on our society...or, like cancer, it will eventually destroy the organism.

CRIMINALITY

According to reports of 2005, The National Institute of Justice found that the five-year recidivism rate in America was 76.6%, and the three-years recidivism rate was 67.8%. The question is: what are we doing wrong as a society that so many of those who have been incarcerated for crimes are back in the prison system instead of living productive and corrected lives? This is a complex question that deserves a serious look since there is so much loss of human resources, potential, and national wealth; by not addressing the problem and seeking a better understanding of what moves a child toward anti-social attitudes and a life of criminality.

On *22 April 2014,* The Bureau of Justice Statistics released: Recidivism of Prisoners in 30 States-Patterns from 2005 to 2010 Update. It reported the following:

- About two-thirds (67.8%) of released prisoners were arrested for a new crime within three years, and three-quarters (76.6%) were arrested within five years.
- Within five years of release, 82.1% of property offenders were arrested for a new crime, compared to 76.9% of drug offenders, 73.6% of public order offenders, and 71.3% of violent offenders.
- More than a third (36.8%) of all prisoners who were arrested within five years of release, were

arrested within the first six months after release, with more than half (56.7%) arrested by the end of the first year.

- A sixth (16.1%) of released prisoners were responsible for almost half (48.4%) of the nearly 1.2 million arrests that occurred in the five-year follow-up period.
- An estimated 10.9% of released prisoners were arrested in a state other than the one that released them during the five-year follow-up period.
- Within five years of release, 84.1% of inmates who were age 24 or younger at release were arrested, compared to 78.6% of inmates aged 25 to 39, and 69.2% of those aged 40 or older.

Punishing someone for a perceived offense, against the established rule, goes back as far as recorded history. The Biblical origin of crime and punishment occurred when God drove Adam and Eve out of the Garden of Paradise, for dis-obeying His rule. I think the gravity of this transgression must have made a very deep impression on all those that came after, because the "sin" of Adam and Eve seems to have had repercussions on all succeeding generations. The concept of justice seems to have been axiomatic in the minds of the ancients as though this was the gold standard of maintaining respect for those in authority, since some sort of order was necessary in sustaining any kind of a tribal or community cohesiveness.

The Code of (King) Hammurabi (1792-1750 BC), of the Babylonian Empire, was perhaps the first official establishment of a set of rules whose obedience was mandatory with punishments relative to a person's status, though there were those that preceded Hammurabi in establishing rules and laws that governed the behavior of the populace and those that ruled them.

Dominique Charpin, a professor at Ecole Pratique des Hautes Etudes, in Paris, in his book, "Writing Law and Kingship in Old Babylonian Mesopotamia" (University of Chicago Press, 2010) states that scholars know of the existence of three law codes, set down by kings, that preceded Hammurabi. The oldest was written by Ur-Nammu, a king of Ur, who reigned from 2094-2111 BC–about three centuries before Hammurabi.

The 300 laws of Hammurabi discussed a wide range of subjects including homicide, assault, divorce, debt, adoption, tradesman's fees, agricultural practices and even disputes regarding the brewing of beer.

(Owen Janus, Live Science Contributor)

A master degree thesis extract by A. J. Van Loon of Leiden University, 2014-12-24, titled: "Law and Order in Ancient Egypt."

The Development of criminal justice from the Pharaonic New Kingdom until the Roman dominate, reported the following:

"In one way or another, the civilizations that ruled over Egypt in antiquity, could all boast a close connection to the concepts of 'law' and 'justice'. Balance, justice and order...all personified by the goddess Ma'at—were cornerstones of Ancient Egyptian religion and society. The Greek Ptolemies, who ruled over Egypt between

323 to 330 BC would become famous for their advanced and intricate bureaucracy, which also featured a highly effective law enforcement system. The Romans, more than any other, prided themselves on their laws, which remain influential in societies to this day. This thesis sets out to discover the way in which criminal justice in Egypt developed from the times of the New Kingdom, through the Ptolemaic era, and under Roman rule."

"Not only for the previously mentioned anecdotal reasons, but the capability to deal with crime and to maintain order can also serve as an indicator for a successful administration, in general." Because criminal law forms an integral part of a legal system in total, which in turn, is inseparable from the general administrative system of a country; they all will be taken into account. The following questions will be answered in this thesis:

"How were the various legal and administrative systems organized?"

"Which actions were thought to be crimes by the Egyptians, Greeks, and Romans? Who possessed the legal authority to deal with such matters? And, in what manner were criminal transgressions dealt with, in practice?" In the end, the aim is to not only find out how criminal justice developed during a period of nearly two millennia, but also, to offer an explanation as to why these developments took their specific course.

The next significant contribution, on issues of crime and punishment, came from the Greeks. In 590 BC, a popular senate legislator by the name of Draco (thus the expression; Draconian law) established some very severe ordinances regarding the administration of justice which persisted until the advent of Roman ascendency in the 1st century AD. With the Greeks, however, there emerged a view of law and order tempered by Philosophical perspectives under the scholarship of Socrates, then Plato and finally Aristotle. There was a great deal of intellectual interest in how natural law, as they saw it, would apply not just to the citizens of Greece but to all humans. Certain classes of humans were disbarred from citizenship, however, such as women, immigrants and slaves.

Meanwhile, in China, India, and the Far East, punishments were very severe or temperate depending on the immediate persuasion of the Emperor. For example, in China there were "five punishments" which prevailed from 2070 thru 1600 BCE under the Xi Dynasty. These punishments involved; amputation of a foot or both feet, amputation of a nose, chiseling or tattooing of the face or forehead, removal of reproductive organs and, finally death. Confucius (479-551 BC), on the other hand, was known for setting ethical models of family and public interactions and setting educational standards and taking a more moderate position on the administration of punishment for transgressions against Imperial law.

(Wikipedia)

As we move into the Roman era (27 BC to 480 AD) in the West, and up to 1453 AD in the East legal development spanned over a thousand years of jurisprudence from the Twelve Tables (449 BC) to the Corpus Juris Civilis (529 AD) as ordered by Justinian I. Roman law formed the basic framework for civil law in Western civilization. The Twelve tables consisted of the following:

I Procedure: For courts and trials
II: Trials continued and theft
III: Debt
IV: Rights of fathers over the family
V: Legal guardianship and inheritance Laws
VI: Acquisition and possession
VII: Land rights and crimes
VIII: Torts and delicts (laws of injury)
IX: Public law
X: Sacred law
XI: Supplement I
XII: Supplement II

The dictum under Justinian I (529-534 AD) established the Corpus Juris Civilis with: Legislation about religion, which mandated the unity of church and state, and anyone not connected to the Christian church was declared a non-citizen; laws against heresy which declared that all must hold the Christian faith. This served as a springboard for international law and which was under the jurisdiction of the Church; and, against paganism which forbid any pagan practices. All persons present at a pagan sacrifice may be indicted as if for murder.

(Wikipedia)

CRIME AND PUNISHMENT UNDER THE EMERGENCE OF CHRISTIANITY

When we look at the emergence of Western Civilization, we must also look at the father of Christianity, i.e. Judaism and the son of Christianity, i.e. Islam, since Christianity emerged from Judaism and Islam emerged from Christianity. It is, also, interesting that the laws pertaining to offensive behavior in all these instances revolved around insults and transgressions against God (Christ being the mediator or savior in Christianity), Yahweh in Judaism and Allah in Islam, rather than against the potentate of civil authority…although in many cases the potentate of a civil jurisdiction was thought of as a god and ruled as such.

So, as we continue with the evolution of criminal jurisprudence in Europe, beginning in the 4th century after the donation of Constantine I, we see the emergence of the Roman Catholic Church in the West and the Eastern Orthodox Church in the East, with institutional dominance in much of the Western and Eastern world. As the Roman Catholic Church gained more power, it developed a harsh administrative dominance over "believers" and "non-believers" such as resulted in the Inquisition that started in 1231, when the Pope Gregory

IX appointed the first "inquisitor of depravity" to quell the antagonistic heretical movements of the time. There are many interpretations of the extent and characteristics of that era of history. The Catholic Church admits that in France and Spain, particularly, there was a severe threat reaction from the Cathars and Waldensians, who opposed the established dogma of the Church as well as the Jews and Moors, who, by that time, had established themselves in Spain and attempted to "pass" as Roman Catholics for the protective services of the realm.

One might ask: "Well, what has all this got to do with the point of this essay?" This vignette of history shows the evolution of harsh, authoritarian dominance over the subjects of kings, rulers, fathers and priests. During this period of European history, under the sovereignty of the Roman Catholic Papacy, even Kings had to bow down to the Holiness of the Pope, and crimes of any kind were considered an affront and insult, not only to the Papacy, but, also, to God Himself. Therefore, crimes of any kind could only be officially admonished and forgiven through the Sacrament of Confession to a priest.

It wasn't until the advent of a Catholic monk by the name of Martin Luther, who, in 1517, opposed the Vatican by displaying in public his 95 theses of protest, that things began to change. Also, around this time King Henry VIII of England dissented with Papal rule and sovereignty over another issue of what, one might say, was his own sovereignty and "right" to marry again whom he pleased. In Luther's case it was, what he saw, were the rights of all people to justify themselves in their understanding of

Christ and, therefore, God. In King Henry's case, it was his insistence to be independent of the rule of the Papacy.

These events seemed to be a watershed time in the history of Western civilization, when the issue of crime and punishment was gradually emerging from crime being thought of as against God but, rather, toward fellow man. This was because an awareness was taking place in the minds of some that ethical responsibilities need not be determined by offenses against the Church but, instead, toward themselves and others. This concept of "self-determination" and the freedom of expression of self, during the Renaissance Period from the 14th to the 17th century, appeared to change the course of human history. Probably, the ultimate culmination of this movement was the French Revolution which lasted from 1789 to 1799, in which a populace insurrection occurred to overthrow the absolute sovereignty of the Kingship of France. However, it was the codified Magna Carta (The Great Charter) of 15 June 1215 in England that set down the establishment of the principle that everyone is subject to the law, even kings, and guarantees the rights of individuals, the right to justice and the right to a fair trial. (Wikipedia)

What appeared to be happening during the political history of Europe between the signing of "The Great Charter" and the end of the French Revolution was an emerging awareness of the responsibility of all humans to determine how they shall be ruled...rather than being ruled by obedience to God through the Papacy of the Church, or obedience to a king through a mandate called the "Divine Rights of Kings."

From the 15th through to the 17th centuries, there was a great movement to expand the economic interests of countries like Spain, Portugal, Netherlands and England, to explore and colonize foreign lands. In 1492 Christopher Columbus was financed by Ferdinand and Isabela of Spain to explore the riches of, what was then called, "The New World." There was also an upsurge of zeal among adventurous souls to find a new way of life and liberty and freedom to practice religion and justice as they saw it. New religious persuasion sprang up following the Protestant Revolution that was started by Martin Luther.

THE COLONIES

When the first pilgrims arrived in Jamestown, VA in 1607, they brought with them the Anglican religion or that of the Church of England, a protestant sect., under King Charles I, along with the laws of dealing with crime and punishment. There were 12 other colonies established from 1607 in Virginia to Georgia in 1732. Each had their unique political and religious structure pertaining to the administration of punishment for transgressions against the established rules of the community. The community was established by the Virginia Company of London and was characterized by strict civil and religious codes of punishment such as:

For cause of undeserved death: starving, hanging, burning, breakage upon the wheel and shooting to death.

For running to the Indians for help: burning.

For stealing to satisfy hunger: hanging from a tree or chained to a tree for starving, whipping, working as slave in irons.

Colonial Crimes and Punishment: James A. Cox

The second colony established was New Hampshire in 1629, which was founded by Capt. John Mason and the Rev. John Millwright who promoted industries of potatoes, fishing, textiles, and ship building. Puritanism was the primary religion but eventually gave way to the Congregational church which included the beliefs of the Quakers and the Baptists. The Puritans led strict religious lives, and dissenters were treated harshly. Then, in 1689, the English Parliament passed the Tolerant Act, which stopped corporal punishment for dissenters, such as chopping the ears of Quakers and whippings for Baptists. This act also freed other religious persuasions to establish churches in Puritan colonies without punishment.

The third colony, what was called New England, was the charter colony of Massachusetts Bay in 1630. The Puritans established a theocratic government with the franchise limited to church members only, The Rev. John.

Cotton and others sought vigorously to prevent independence of other religious views. Puritans sought to "purify" the Church of England from its "Catholic" practices, maintaining that the Church of England was only partially reformed. Massachusetts Bay colony was also noted for prosecuting crimes of moral offenses more so than crimes against persons or property. Crimes against the government were considered more severe than those against people of lower status. Individuals with black skin were thought to be strange and exotic, evil and satanic creatures and were treated mercilessly.

Crime and Punishment in Colonial Times
Obert C. Twombly and Robert H. Moore,
Apr. 1967.

The next colony to be established among the 13
original was the colony of Maryland in 1632. The intent
of Lord Baltimore was to provide a safe haven for English
Catholics in the New World at the time of the European
wars of religious strife among Anglicans, Puritans,
Catholics, and Quakers. Lord Baltimore was later removed
and replaced by a Protestant, Charles Calvert.

As in all other jurisdictions of colonial policy there
was always an undertone of religious moral transgression
and, such transgressions were deemed to be a severe threat
to the stability and integrity of the community.

Both Connecticut and Rhode Island were established
in 1636 as charter colonies. In both cases a group of people
were led by such as:

Roger Williams who purchased land from the
Narragansett Indians, to establish the Rhode Island
colony in Providence. A similar situation occurred with
Connecticut. The rules and ordinances were similar in
that such were administered with guidelines set up by
religious factions. In this case also, it was of the Puritan
persuasion. The remaining six colonies: Delaware in
1638, Carolina in 1653, New Jersey, New York in 1664,
Pennsylvania in 1682, and Georgia in 1732 had similar
beginnings with very harshly imposed punishments
under the aegis of the religious constabulary. However,
since religiosity in the administration of justice tended to
be rather severe and debilitating there were undercurrents

of discontent that eventually found their way into our Constitution and Bill of Rights which stressed the separation of Church and State, following the American Revolutionary War of 1776.

THE DEVELOPMENT OF CRIMINAL JUSTICE IN AMERICA

As a result, the notion of imprisonment and separation from society became a more enlightened approach to the administration of crime and punishment along with the prospect of correction but that has not shown to be an effective solution with reference to the great recidivism rate in America, today.

The great question, then, seems to be: How can we, as a progressive and vital society, deal with those who transgress our peace and order? How can justice be administered humanely and with an understanding that will enable one so disinclined toward amiable society with his fellow man to be truly reset on a more viable course of life?

In the 19th century there emerged the "due process mode" and the "crime control model." The origin of the due process model originally came from the clause 39 of the Magna Carta in which "No man shall be arrested or imprisoned except by lawful judgement of his peers or the law of the land." The "crime control model" on the other hand, allegedly began with the origin of the first modern police force with the Metropolitan Police Force in London in 1829 by Sir Robert Peel. The Peelian Principles, as they were called, were developed as a deterrent to urban crime and disorder. This was followed by the US in 1838 in which Boston, and then New York City in 1844, followed suit. However, the police were not respected because corruption was rampant. In 1920 in Berkeley, California police chief August Vollmer and O.W. Wilson began to professionalize, adopt new technologies and place emphasis on training and professional qualifications of new hires.

(Wikipedia)

The "Crime control model" refers to a theory of criminal justice which places emphasis on reducing crime in society through increased police and prosecutorial powers. In contrast, the "due process model" focuses on individual liberties and rights and is concerned with limiting the powers of government. We can, therefore, see that behind this political fugue was the conflict between self-determination and "police" powers of the King and the Papacy in Europe. This dichotomous way of thinking (due process vs crime control models) with respect to criminal behavior presented, in practice, as the legalities, on the one hand, and the administration of justice on the other.

As the population in the US grew and the incidence of crime also increased, the court dockets expanded to an unmanageable level, and "A fast and speedy trial" was no longer feasible. As a result, Plea bargaining has served as compensatory dispositions, even in some serious cases, by reducing a felony to a misdemeanor. Moreover, the courts are literally overwhelmed with those being brought to trial for drug abuse problems and crimes associated with it. Police are overwhelmed because of the sheer volume and seriousness of criminal behavior. The police also get frustrated because so often those who risk their lives to apprehend criminal offenders, find that the offenders are soon released from custody and back on the streets.

As a former deputy juvenile probation officer, myself, in the 1960s, I have seen the character of crime committed by juvenile go from petty theft, malicious mischief and joy- riding, to carrying guns and knives to school and, in some cases, using these weapons against fellow students and even teachers. The precursor to more serious crimes on the part of juveniles were those cases called "Beyond the control and supervision" of parents, because parents were too busy struggling to earn a living and consequently relinquished their authority to the school, the church, and any other institution that was mandated by law to step in including the juvenile probation officer. Parents would often come into the office saying, "I get no respect from my kid. He won't listen to me and won't obey me. You (the juvenile probation officer) take charge." When children do not get the attention and developmental support they need, it become axiomatic that they will get into trouble with the law or with themselves. Psychologists will say that when the emotional needs of children are not met, they will either act out against society (usually in groups or gangs) or against themselves in emotional disorders or self-mutilation. When this all happened in the'60s, the result was the great juvenile/tribal movement which opened the door to the massive drugs and homeless problems that we had not seen before. This was the era of "Tune in, turn on and drop out," as promoted by the Harvard psychology professor, Timothy Leary. Educational standards have declined, relative to the demand for increased competitiveness in the technical global marketplace, resulting in fewer young people being prepared for adult responsibilities. Many juveniles have landed in custody because they have chosen to resort to the hopeless venture of criminality, and many were found to have been so poorly educated that they were able to read only at a third-grade level.

The term precedent is often used in court proceedings and is traditionally built on the doctrine of Stare Decisis ("Stand by decided matters"), which directs a court to look to past decisions, for guidance, on how to decide a case before it. This means that the legal rules applied to a prior case, with facts that are similar to those of the case now before a court, should be applied to resolve the legal dispute. There are, undoubtedly, real values in the use of precedent such as: providing predictability, stability, and efficiency. It also gives a sense that the law is just since similar judgements are handed down which conform to similar cases in the past. However, it could also be argued that the use of precedent can impose a dependent rigidity on the administration of justice because as the law tends to remain fixed, human evolution moves on. The rule of law must also be able to grow and change as human awareness and mindfulness becomes more cognizant of its individual and social responsibilities. This essay attempts to show the evolutionary character of human progress and the need to regard it from a criminal justice point of view.

The issue "Rowe vs Wade" is a case in point. Since 1973, the right to life has been a hot item in the courts, and among the population of sensitive people. It wasn't too long ago when very few considered the right to life of an unborn fetus as a serious issue except perhaps for the girl who may have become inadvertently pregnant and had to seek out the services of a clandestine abortion clinic. The Catholic Church took the position that life began at the moment of conception and therefore any interference with the gestation process was forbidden by the laws of nature and God. Now, people store their embryos cryogenically for future use. Even though artificial birth control is also prohibited by Papal decree, approx. 85% of Catholics in the US practice birth control, as documented by Catholic Priest and Professor of Sociology, at Chicago University, Andrew Greeley, now deceased.

Another issue for discussion is the MADD movement. It is estimated that in the year 2015, 10265 individuals died as a result of alcohol impaired driver crashes. This is a significant drop from earlier figures because there was a forced awareness of the responsibility of drivers not to drive when they are impaired from intoxication. The litigation against drunk driving came in 2004, as a result of the work of Candace Lightner whose 13-year old daughter, Cari, was killed (*5 Sept. 1980*) by a drunk driver, establishing in every State an alcohol limit of 0.08 BAC. Drivers are now held responsible whereas drunk driving, before legislation, was considered a minor offense even if the intoxicated driver caused the accident. It was thought that an intoxicated driver was not fully aware or conscious of what he was doing by driving drunk. The point being that the administration of criminal justice must become more adaptable to the growing awareness of the populace.

Administering justice for the errant and anti-social, must regard the rights and liberties of individuals and, at the same time, protect the peace and order of the society as a whole. An important point to remember and I am sure would be endorsed by our founding fathers is that responsibility comes for rights and liberties. Living in a democratic republic, like ours, requires that all of us hold our citizenship with pride, dignity and respect for the principles upon which it was founded.

Throwing people into jails and prisons for transgressions against the law has not proven to be effective. Rehabilitation and correction are high sounding words, but they don't work with most people because by the time a person reaches adulthood, he or she has developed a character which is hard to change. We are not dealing with the problem early enough at a time when an individual is in the process of developing his or her character. The notion of equating "time served" for a specific transgression is a very outmoded idea. It completely ignores the concept of socialization and instead thinks only of punishment as the only corrective measure. So, instead of wasting human resources and squandering the potential talents and contributions of our less fortunate citizens, let's take a look at something new that might offer a way of saving our civilization rather than destroying it.

A NEW CRIMINAL JUSTICE MODEL IN AMERICA

There was a time in America when the police were respected and looked up to, much like a teacher or other professionals. A cop walked a beat in a neighborhood and had a re-assuring smile. He knew his people in the neighborhood and they knew him. If a child committed a delinquent act, the local police officer would talk to him in a fair, firm and friendly way and then return him to his parents with a slight admonishment so the parents could apply some discipline. Children often learn to respect the police as representatives of the community. It seems we have gotten away from the concept of neighborhood and community policing. The best policing was done on the child's own territory, such as the school or recreational facility.

Moving to an even more basic consideration of human resources is to take a look at how a person develops; what are the needs, motivations and sequential tasks each child must experience as their character is formed? Abraham Maslow has presented interesting studies about needs and motivations as a child grows to adulthood.

From the Journal of General Psychology, 1945, 33, 21-41– a study was conducted by A.H. Maslow, Elisa Hirsh, Marcella Stein, and Irma Honigmann, titled: "A Clinically Derived Test for Measuring Psychological

Security-Insecurity" and it was described by means of the following table.

Insecurity	Security
1. Feelings of being rejected or being unloved, or being treated coldly and without affection, or being hated, or being despised.	1. Feelings of being liked or being acceptance or being locked upon with warmth.
2. Feeling of isolation, ostracism, aloneness or being out of it.	2. Feeling of belongingness of being at home in the world, or not feeling threatened.
3. Perception of the world and life as dangerous, threatening, dark, or hostile or challenging; as every man's action are against the other.	3. Perception as pleasant, warm, friendly and a benevolent place.
4. Perception of other human beings essentially bad evil, or self-centered, as dangerous, threatening, hostile or challenging, constant feeling of threat and anxiety.	4. Perception of human beings as essentially good, warm, friendly or benevolent. Feeling of safety and un-anxious.

5. Feeling of mistrust, envy or jealousy toward others; much hostility, prejudices and hatred	5. Feeling of friendliness and trust in others, little hostility, tolerance of others or easy affection for others
6. Tendency to expect the worst and general pessimism.	6. Tendency to expect good to happen and general optimism,

Maslow outlined a set of needs that each child is motivated to have gratified in a rank order of ascendency from:

Basic needs:
- Physiological: Food, water, warmth and rest
- Safety: Security

Psychological needs:
- Belongingness: Love, intimate relationships and friends.
- Esteem or self-valuing: Prestige and feelings of accomplishment and competence.
- Self-fulfilment needs:
- Self-Actualization: Achieving one's full potential including creative activities.

According to Maslow, if these needs are thwarted or denied, what prevails in the development of the child is a pathological perception of threat i.e., the world is not a safe and friendly place to be, and this leads to the features of "insecurity" listed above.

Along a similar line of thinking are the developmental tasks as outlined by Erik Erikson as follows:

- Stage one. HOPE: trust vs mistrust (oral-sensory, infancy, zero-two years)

Existential Question: Can I trust the world?

- Stage two. WILL: autonomy vs shame and doubt (early childhood, two-four years)

Existential Question: Is it OK to be me?

- Stage three. PURPOSE: Initiative vs guilt (locomotor, preschool, four-five yrs.)

Existential Question: Is it OK for me to do, move and act?

- Stage four. COMPETENCE: Industry vs inferiority (school age, 5-12 yrs.)

Existential Question: Can I make it in the world of people?

- Stage five. FIDELITY and Authenticity: Identity vs role confusion (adolescence, 13-19 yrs.)

Existential Question: Who am I and what can I be?

- Stage six. LOVE: Intimacy vs isolation (early adulthood, 20-39 yrs.)

Existential Question: Can I love?

- Stage seven. CARE: generativity vs stagnation (adulthood, 40-64 yrs.)

Existential Question: Can I make my life count?

- Stage eight. WISDOM: ego integrity vs despair (maturity. 65-death)

Existential Question: Is it OK to have been me?

When a young child has not successfully passed through the early stages of development, assisted by an adequate gratification of basic needs and motivations, we find a frustration and hopelessness, and a seeking out of drugs and alternative compensation, to fill the void of anomie and despair. This is what we see every day in the news about the mayhem and disorder in our society. This is what lands potentially creative and productive individuals in jails and prisons — many of whom are simply wasted lives. This is not to say that all those that suffer inadequate development are destined not to reach higher ground, but it takes extraordinary effort and external support to make that happen. The "Bird Man of Alcatraz" was a case in point. Here was a man who was sentenced to a purposeless life, locked in a cell for a crime he committed in his youth at the age of 19, but was determined to create some meaning to his life by contributing to science through a study of the diseases of birds. He apparently wanted to show to the world, and to himself, that he had some value, and was competent to do something of some importance.

A sense of competence is so important to the development of a young person; it establishes, whether, a boy or girl will find contributory satisfaction in life or a futile sense of inadequacy and failure to thrive.

Ann S. Masten and J. Douglas Coatsworth present in the American Psychologist, Feb. 1998, a study titled, "The Development of Competence in Favorable and Unfavorable Environments," Lessons from Research on Successful Children.

They say: "The development of competence holds great interest for parents and society alike. This article considers implications from research on competence and resilience in children and adolescents for establishing policy and interventions, designed to foster better outcomes among children at risk. Foundations of competence in early development are discussed, focusing on the role of attachment relationships and self-regulation. Results from studies of competence in the domains of peer relations, conduct, school, work and activities are highlighted. Lessons are drawn from studies of naturally occurring resilience among children at risk because of disadvantages or trauma and, also, from efforts to deliberately alter the course of competence through early childhood education and preventive interventions. Converging evidence suggests that the same powerful adaptive systems protect development in both favorable and unfavorable environments."

The conclusions drawn from this study are as follows: "Studies of competence, resilience, and intervention converge to suggest that there are powerful adaptive systems that foster and protect the development of competence in favorable and unfavorable environments. These systems are manifest in the quality of parent-child attachments, cognition, and self-regulation. Children who do well, have adults who care for them, brains that are developing normally, and, as they grow older, the ability to manage their own attention, emotions, and behavior. These adaptive systems also mutually enhance each other in the course of development. Undoubtedly, there are other protective processes that promote competence. But these three sets of processes clearly play a central role in multiple domains of competence. Poverty, chronic stress, domestic violence, natural disasters, and other high-risk contexts for child development may have lasting effects when they damage or impair these crucial adaptive systems; effective preventive interventions may work by bolstering or restoring these systems."

Time and again, research points to the importance of parent-child relationships as a crucial context for the development of competence, both, for children with ordinary lives and for children facing extraordinary challenges. In US society, the combination of warm, structured child-rearing practices in parents with reasonably high expectations for competence is strongly tied to success in multiple domains and to resilience among children at risk. In extremely dangerous environments, effective parents are likely to be strict but remain warm and caring. When a parent, like this, is not available in a child's life, competence is often linked to a surrogate care-giving figure who serves a mentoring role. When adversity is high and no effective adult is connected to a child, risk for maladaptation is high. The development of competence requires the involvement of a caring, competent adult in a child's life; ensuring that every child has the fundamental protective system is a policy imperative.

A second broad and salient predictor of competence is good cognitive development or intellectual functioning. Perhaps, because of the complexity of human brain development and functioning, processes underlying the connection of good cognitive skills to competence are not entirely clear.

Nonetheless, generally good cognitive skills predict not only academic achievement but other aspects of competence, as well, such as rule-abiding behavior. It is possible that self-regulation skills account for some of the power of IQ scores to predict competence and resilience.

Children who have trouble directing their attention or controlling their impulses may not do well on IQ tests or in the classroom or may not learn to comply with rules as readily or get along well with peers. On the other hand, children with good cognitive skills may be better equipped to handle the cognitive load inherent in adverse situations. In any case, policies and programs to protect and foster good cognitive development are essential for building human capital.

Self-regulation of attention, emotion, and behavior comprise a third major set of adaptation skills implicated as central to the development of competence across domains and modifiable through experience, particularly in early development. Moreover, good parent-child relationships serve as scaffolds for building these skills. Intervening early, to encourage self-regulation, may be an important strategy for future interventions, although we need to know more about these processes to inform such efforts.

Studies of competence, psychopathology and resilience all point to the importance of establishing a good start early in development. Children who enter school with significant problems in self-regulation, are distrustful of adults, or with impaired learning abilities, have a substantial disadvantage for meeting the developmental tasks of middle childhood.

Cascading effects are also suggested by the literature highlighted here. Children who have good internal and external resources tend to get off to a good start in school, become connected to normative peers, maintain positive self-perceptions, and face the developmental tasks of adolescence with the advantages represented by success in these domains. Children who enter school with few resources, cognitive difficulties, and self-regulatory problems often have academic problems, get into trouble with teachers, are more likely to be rejected by peers, and are at risk of disengaging from normative school and peer contexts, which sets them up for considerable difficulty in the transition to adolescence.

Prevention, at its best, represents both an effort to foster competence, and to prevent problems. Intervention can be conceptualized as a protective process by which one deliberately attempts to steer development in more favorable directions. Increasingly, interventions are designed on the basis of research– on competence and resilience as well as on psychopathology. Experimental evaluations of interventions, designed on the basis of theory and research, represent a powerful strategy for testing causal hypotheses, which will serve to improve our theories and also to fine-tune preventive intervention programs. It is in the common interest of society and science that evaluations of well-designed interventions go forward.

The study of competence and resilience offers hope and guidance for those who seek to improve the odds of good developmental outcomes, through policy and prevention. Children do make it in spite of adversity, and research on efforts to reduce risk, boost resources, and facilitate protective processes is encouraging. At the same time, there is growing respect for the complexity of the processes that influence the course of human development and the challenge of implementing change in the dynamic systems in which children develop.

Future studies undoubtedly will advance our understanding of the many possible pathways to competence. Rapid growth in our knowledge, about brain development, will contribute to our understanding of competence processes, as will advances in the knowledge of how self-regulation systems develop. The role of culture in the development of competence, is also receiving greater and much-needed attention. Longitudinal studies should help us to determine, how trauma and adversity may alter the course of development? and what kind of protective systems are needed to prevent long-term negative consequences of trauma exposure or to promote recovery? Multidisciplinary research will make it possible to integrate biological, psychological, anthropological and sociological perspectives, on adaption in development.

Research has illuminated the lives of successful children in times of growing concerns about the effects of poverty, homelessness, maltreatment, domestic and community violence, educational failure and teen pregnancy. Successful children remind us that children grow up in multiple contexts, in families, schools, peer groups, baseball teams, religious organizations, and many other groups, and each context is a potential source of protective factor as well as risks. These children demonstrate that children are protected not only by the self-righting nature of development but also by the actions of adults, by their own actions, by the nurturing of their assets, by opportunities to succeed and by the experiences of success. The behavior of adults often plays a critical role in children's risks, resources, opportunities and resilience. Development is biased toward competence but there is no such thing as an invulnerable child. If we allow the prevalence of known risk factors' development to rise while resources for children fall, we can expect the competence of individual children and the human capital of the nation to suffer.

Jeremy Glenesk studied criminal justice in several countries around the world, at Mount Royal University in Calgary, Alberta, in Feb. 2016. He presented his findings as follows: "Norway is considered (there is some debate, due to varying systems of measurement worldwide because some agencies define recidivism as re-arrest while others look at a new conviction upon release) to have, one of the lowest recidivism rates in the world. Why is this? Many would argue that their system works so well because they treat offenders as actual people, rather than as a tumor that needs to be excised from society. You can find plenty of articles on Google, and pictures of their prisons, and many people from other nations would laugh and think it's a joke. Their prisons are pristine. They look like a country club. Offenders in some Norwegian prisons can go horseback riding, and often have televisions, gyms, and kitchens. Their system seeks to remove their freedom, and nothing else. They live a healthy and normal lifestyle while in prison but are simply unable to leave. Their system seeks to actively rehabilitate offenders back into society by teaching them skills and finding them work upon re-entry into society."

I might add, that this way of thinking uses a reward system as a motivator rather than punishment. Prisoners are deprived of privileges for non-compliance and rewarded with special privileges for compliance and acceptable contributions to the well-being of all.

"So how does Norway accomplish this feat? The country relies on a concept called 'restorative justice', which aims to repair the harm caused by crime rather than punish people. This system focuses on rehabilitating prisoners. Taking a look at Halden prison you'll see what we mean. The 75-acre facility maintains as much 'normalcy' as possible. That means no bars on the widows, kitchens fully equipped with sharp objects, and friendships between guards and inmates. For Norway, removing people's freedom is enough of a punishment." And the fact that the recidivism rate is so low testifies to the fact that freedom is more valued than incarceration, even with the best of living conditions. The maximum life sentence is 21 years with five-year extensions for special cases if the prisoner does not accept rehabilitation. As Hoidel Halden, prison Director, puts it: "Our goal is that, every inmate in Norwegian prison is going back to the society. Do you want people who are angry or people who are rehabilitated?"

It could be argued that those who are the most intractable are those who have experienced extreme emotional deprivation as small children and, consequently, never learned to trust or see the world as a friendly place. Question: Is it possible to re-generate trust in an adult whose character has been formed without it?

For those that are most intractable, a suggestion that on the face of it, sounds barbaric, cruel and unusual punishment might on second thought, seem more humane when looked at from the point of view of true rehabilitation. When someone develops cataracts of the eyes and loses vision, an ophthalmologist will remove the diseased lenses and then replace them with artificial ones, which restores vision. If one were to remain without the lenses for a time they would be required to depend on or trust someone in order to exercise any effective ambulation. For those without criminal records, getting around is a laborious task even with a seeing eye dog, and their freedoms are considerable curtailed. With someone who is imprisoned, having lost their vision but with the hope of regaining it again could serve as a strong motivational reward for attitude re-adjustment. Perhaps the pros. and cons. of such an idea could be the subject of serious discussion among those whose job is to truly rehabilitate prisoners.

Since this essay is about addressing the problem of not only recidivism in the US criminal justice system but the incidence of crime and violence in the society in general and why some people are inclined toward crime and social disorder in the first place?

Referring to a study written up by Denise C. Gottfredson, David B. Wilson and Stacy Skroban Najaka, titled; Evidence-Based Crime Prevention-School Based Crime Prevention, published by Routledge in 2002, we have the following findings:

"Schools have great potential as a locus for crime prevention. They provide regular access to students throughout the developmental years, and perhaps the only consistent access to large numbers of the most crime-prone young children in the early school years. The schools are staffed with individuals paid to help youth develop as healthy, happy, productive citizens and the community usually support schools' efforts to socialize youth."

Factors which are considered precursors of delinquency, as identified by research, are the following: Characteristics of school and classroom-related environments as well as individual-related school-related experiences, personal values, attitudes and beliefs.

School environmental factors related to delinquency include availability of drugs, alcohol and weapons. School related experiences and attitudes, which often precede delinquency, include poor school performance and attendance, low feeling of attachment to the school and education at all. Other contributing factors are: Peer rejection, bullying, impulsiveness and associating with delinquent peers, and a pervading low self-esteem.

Individual factors contributing toward delinquent behavior are rebellious attitudes and beliefs favoring law violations and low levels of social competency skills such as identifying likely consequences of choices.

In addressing the problem of improving the school experience, as a corrective approach to the growing phenomenon of crime and disorder in our society, we must look at the three most important institutions for raising healthy, happy and purposeful children: The family, the school and the neighborhood or community. There is ample evidence-based research to support this contention. If we want to preserve our way of life, we must focus on the progeny of America, those who will take over after each generation.

Here, I would like to refer to my first writings in this area titled: "How goes it With America in the Interests of Educational Reform." This book is currently undergoing revision and re-publication and will also be on the market in the spring of 2018.

THE FAMILY AS A BULWARK AGAINST DELINQUENCY AND SOCIAL DISORDER

Nothing beats an emotionally warm, stable, and attentive home for the successful rearing of children. The quality of parenting in the US appears to have declined in the last 50 years or so. This is partly due to economic and political changes as well as the advent of social diversions. There was a time after WWII, when a young father was able to get a secure job which paid enough to support his family with a house, a car and enough money for health services and recreation and even to offer helping support for tuitions for college that were exceedingly affordable. Mothers were able to stay home and attend to the needs and character building of their small children and there was mutual support between parents and teachers. This is no longer the case today since most young parents must both works, even if there are two parents in the home which often is not the case, just to make ends meet. The children often go unsupervised and neglected. Stability in the home is now available to only a few who are fortunate enough to be highly endowed with wealth. Higher education, today, is virtually prohibited for many of the deserving young people, because of inordinate costs.

Youngsters need all the elements of security mentioned above by Maslow, Erikson, Masten and Coatsworth, and others whose studies clearly show that elements of growth and maturity follow the pattern of gratification and achievement of needs, developmental tasks and competency. Parents need to be mature and competent, themselves, so they can provide the environmental and emotional structure that will foster healthy development.

The following is a parable of a boy named Mitch who was like any precious, incomparable child, a million-dollar diamond in the rough. For the first few years of his life, Mitch only knew himself from the reflections he saw of himself in the eyes of his caretakers. Even though his caretakers were not blind, they saw him through the kaleidoscope of their own perceptions, needs and expectations. Consequently, even though his caretakers were always present, not one of them ever actually saw him as he was, as he attempted to emerge as the person he was meant to be. By the time he was grown up, he knew himself only as a mosaic of other people's images of him. No one had ever really seen him or reflected back to him who he really was or looked like. As a result, he thought he was the mosaic of images. Sometimes in the dark of night when he was all alone, Mitch knew that something of profound importance was missing. He experienced a gnawing sense of emptiness, a deep void. He tried to fill the emptiness and void with many things: accomplishments, money, status, prestige, food, sex, adventure, travel, marriages, children, excitement, work and even exercise. But no matter what he did he never felt the gnawing emptiness go away. In the quiet of the night when all the distractions were gone, he heard a still quiet voice that said: "Don't forget; please don't forget me" But, alas! Mitch did forget and went to his death never knowing who he was. This is the tragic story of those who are raised by incompetent parents or caregivers.

How children perceive themselves and the world depends so much? How people close to them relate to them? A case in point, is the FLDS cult presided over by Warren Jeffs (who had numerous wives and children and claimed to be a prophet) who was convicted and imprisoned in 2011 on two felony counts of child sexual assault, and even to this day he controls his cult members from within his prison cell.

There was a time in our history, when children were produced and exploited primarily to help with the economic security of the family or to be exploited by commercial industry and we have come to recognise that this was an unjust exploitation of the child. Children have rights as well as adults. They have a right to "life, liberty and their own pursuit of happiness" as stated in our own Constitution. They have a right to be respected and honored and taught that in our society, which is a democratic republic, that each person has a responsibility toward themselves and to others in the sustaining and perpetuation of this way of life. With rights go privileges, and also responsibilities. The responsibilities we talk of, speak to the importance and value of developing one's potential capabilities so they can enjoy the satisfaction that comes with successful accomplishment for themselves, and also the inherent gratification and gratitude that comes from serving others with what you have to offer.

Parents need to spend enough time with their children so they can enjoy them and be sensitive enough to reflect back to them what interests and excites them. In other words, parents must be emotionally supportive and in tune with their children while, at the same time, making sure children learn to do for themselves and strive for confident independence. That's the job of parents. A highly recommended book on how to inspire values in children is titled: "Children Learn What They Live" by Dorothy Law Nolte. For example, she writes: "If children live with criticism, they learn to condemn, if children live with acceptance, they learn to love."

It is the contention of many that the rights of children are severely violated, and grave injustice is done when children are produced by the irresponsible and immature. It is for this reason that much more ought to be done in the schools and by parents in teaching the responsibilities and hardships of parenthood as well as the delights and satisfactions of raising a child. I would go so far as to advocate that prospective parents be given formal tests to determine if they are qualified for parenthood. We test for admittance to special schools and higher education, for police and public safety, for driving, we test for qualifying professional people and just about everything except the most important function of our society, the raising of children.

Frustration of children's needs, love and attention, lead to resentment and aggression, which is often turned inward toward the self and inhibits the child's need for emotional growth and development. As John Dollard, the American psychologist, puts it, "The existence of frustration always leads to some form of aggression. This holds for all needs. The more central and essential the need whose gratification is thwarted, the more intense the resulting hostility and aggression are likely to be." Dr Karen Horney, author of "The Neurotic Personality of our Time" wrote, "The main reason why a child does not receive enough warmth and affection lies in the parents' incapacity to give it on account of their own neuroses." This is what Dr Horney termed "The basic evil" in our time "The lack of genuine warmth and affection." Quoting Samuel J. Warner, Ph.D. in his book, Self-Realization and Self Defeat, he states, "The thing that often tips the balance away from self-realization and toward self-defeat is this: Unconscious resentment builds up in the individual to a point at which he can no longer contain himself, and in one form or another the underlying resentment, to some degree, breaks through as self-defeat."

"My thesis is that the job of parents is to be there for children. This is why I wouldn't allow anyone under 30 to have a child. I'd also have extensive mental health tests and child-bearing instruction be pre-requisites for parenting. Since there is a fat chance that this will ever happen, no one need worry about me getting my way. I'm 50 now and I'm ready to be a parent, I think."— John Bradshaw

THE SCHOOL AS A BULWARK AGAINST DELINQUENCY AND SOCIAL DISORDER

When a child first enters the school system, it is now possible to give each child a thorough and comprehensive readiness evaluation not only for readiness for school but also an assessment of the child health and developmental milestones, social and domestic background and any other factors that would deter the child being able to successfully matriculate into the educational process. This is the time in a child's life when it is so important for teachers and parents to be sensitive to any pathological traits that may be developing in a child. This is the time when corrective measures can be most effective. We wonder why some individuals in a fit of rage will cause terrible violence and destruction as an adult. It is the result of accumulated distress over years of unfulfilled needs and gratifications during the developmental years. Addressing the needs of these young people at the early stage of their development is, to a large extent, the work of the professional school psychologist assisted by the primary care givers, school personnel and other professionals.

It would also be suggested that the grades, from k through three, be ungraded so that children can be entered at their readiness levels, be individualized by the teacher and remain so until ready for 4th grade. Some children are ready at the age of four and others not until they are six-years old. Furthermore, even though competition is a valued endeavor in our society it is not productive for very small children to feel they are competing with other children for grades or recognition. They must only be encouraged to excel at whatever they show an interest and propensity for. In other words, to compete with themselves in attempting to master whatever they do. In addition, grading should not be competitive at the early stages of development. So, instead of an "a, b, c, d, e, and f" grading system, a grading system of pass, superior or incomplete should be adopted as recommended by William Glasser in his book, schools without failure. Those with special gifts ought to be encouraged to do special projects that they want to do and present their results to the class instead of advancing beyond their peers and classmates. Advancement, if necessary, can be done at higher grade levels if warranted. In this regard it is also important that those who are gifted, be recognized and dealt with accordingly so as not to stifle their inherent, intensity, complexity and drive.

Early school experiences for a child are very important in setting a lifelong attitude towards education and learning and that is why the teachers at those lower levels must be specially trained and qualified not only in teaching skills for small children but knowledge of the pedagogy of child development. A hyper-critical teacher can severely dampen the natural enthusiasm for learning. A warm, intelligent and encouraging teacher can make all the difference in the development of a child's attitude toward learning and toward his/her own self-concept of competence and attitude toward learning. We want to be sure that each child, by the time he/she finishes those early four years (K-3) is well grounded in the basics of reading, writing and arithmetic and successful socialization.

When a child enters 4th grade, this is the time to start introducing the elements of the immediate community (the services of the police, firefighters, libraries, medical personnel and all those connected with public service) in which he/she lives and extending that to the broad concept of nationhood and, for that matter, the world community at large. Also, the reality of competitiveness, as an incentive toward excellence in production and self-development, can be introduced as an assertive disposition, not as a hostile or aggressive attitude. There should never be hostile/competitive bullying or discriminating prejudices in the schools.

Problems like this ought to be handled by the school counselor. Sadly, many schools are not equipped with well trained counselors. Unfortunately, counselors are often frustrated at being assigned administrative tasks that occupy much their time.

Formal curricula in many schools are sadly lacking in not only socialization skills but in the practical aspects of living. This, it seems to me, is an important part of educating the young in their progress toward adulthood. In other words, "Why re-invent the wheel," as the old saying goes. Why not give children a heads-up on how to matriculate into the adult world? Let's give them the benefit of our experience and what we have learned as adults.

At the high school level, much more emphasis ought to be placed in a child's endeavor to successfully achieve the developmental task of identity and social competence. This is where the services of the professional counselor become so important. In addition to the basic subjects of the high school curriculum, the teen-ager must come to know who they are? and how to relate themselves to the "world of work," and the adult world in general? It is a very complex and competitive world they are about to inherit, and they should be given the knowledge and skills necessary to navigate successfully in this modern world of today. They must know about how to form effective and meaningful relationships? how to make their contribution to their society? how to handle their money and negotiate through the complex world of finance and housing? how to take care of their health and wellbeing as they grow older? and how to deal with discouragement and failure, and that will inevitably happen as well. There ought to be discussions about values not just one's own but those of the society and world in which they live so they can make some choices about what works and what doesn't. As adults they are going to have to make choices about how and where they want to live and work? who they want to mate with? who they want to lead them? and how they want their economy to run? These are all very practical questions that teen-agers want answered. Without this guidance it become a very anxious and depressing outlook for their future.

In our educational history, teachers were respected and admired members of the community. They were regarded as professionals and the respect was relayed through the parents by their children, and when a child was reprimanded in the school, the parent often backed up the teacher unless there was some blatant misbehavior on the part of the school official. In that case the educator was either reprimanded or dismissed before the advent of tenure. The issue of tenure has many pros. and cons., but the abuses can have serious consequences for good teachers and the quality of education for children.

Many of us including school officials themselves attest that tenure in the lower grades poses complex problems because it serves as a haven for incompetent and uninspired people who do not have the talent or inspiration to be a quality teacher. This has a detrimental effect on the morale of good teachers, and it seriously hampers the effectiveness of a child's educational experience. Tenure at the college or university level made some sense because it was thought that people at that level of education were mature enough to use their own judgement as to the ideas and persuasions of their professors; because professors ought to have the freedom to express their own opinions and thoughts. However, the younger students are still in the process of developing their characters, and therefore it is imperative that teachers be more concerned about teaching the fundamental values and purposes of this nation as well as what this nation stands for. Too many children, today, are very unclear as to what this country does stand for.

Young people have a great deal of idealism, energy and enthusiasm and, also a desire to assume some meaningful responsibility. This, also, ought to be part of the high school program in which seniors have an opportunity to engage in a study experience of their liking, so they can learn, under supervision, what it is like to actually hold a job and come to work on time. This can be a supplemental activity for half a day. I did this in Brazil when I was the guidance counselor at an American school in Recife and it worked out well.

I am also persuaded that, in terms of student morale and self-respect, the school ought to establish not only rules of conduct, but rules of dress and rules pertaining to driving cars to school. Driving a car is a privilege, not a right and ought to be regarded as such by the school administration; so, this ought to be a seniors' privilege particularly if he/she has responsibilities that warrant the use of a car. Students as well as teachers must have a healthy respect for themselves and their institution of learning.

An old axiom among psychologists is that you can't start solving a problem until you first acknowledge that it exists. With reference to the school systems in America, it does appear that there is a resistance to acknowledging shortcomings and making changes that will adapt to the challenges of the 21st century. In the past children were regimented into a lock-step rote learning mode that was suitable for employment in a manufacturing economy. A worker could offer his skills with loyalty to a company and be well assured of a job throughout his working life; with a gold watch and reliable pension upon retirement. That type of employment is becoming rare, and the schools must be re-configured to meet the skill demands of the 21st century labor market. The world is becoming more interactive and complex every day. In order for a democratic republic like ours to prevail, the populace must be educated to understand the real issues confronting the society. In earlier days, the populace, in their wisdom, alleged that a well-educated society was a more effective society and so it was deemed appropriate that all children should be entitled to a free public education up through high school because very few went on to college. Today, the complexity of the world requires more extensive education so that a college education is more equivalent to a high school education in former days. Therefore, education up through college ought to be made accessible for a minimal and affordable cost to all deserving students. Trade schools and apprenticeships for those not academically inclined should be made available as well as schools for the arts and crafts as it is in New York City.

Since education is also a matter of building character in the young it is important that teachers and educators meet higher professional standards of effectiveness, much like all professions. That would include such qualities as creating a friendly classroom atmosphere, establishing a feeling of security, exerting a stabilizing influence, inspiring originality, initiative and developing self-reliance.

Tenure at the elementary and secondary levels ought to be re-considered for the sake of keeping an edge on the effectiveness of teachers, and ensuring that those who are not in keeping with standards of excellence should be let go and guided toward other occupations more suitable to their interests and skills.

The public-school system must rededicate itself to the noble purpose of enhancing communal attitudes of good will and connectedness and building confidence and trust in the American way of life. Community leaders must promote social-ethical values in the workplace such as flextime, in-house childcare, maternity and paternity leave, counseling for those that must be re-assigned or have need for resolving personal crises, work-out facilities and healthy lunch counters. In addition, coordinating with the high schools in the process of matriculating young people into the labor market, so they can be assured of suitable training and direction in the interests of a more synergistic work environment, is an absolute necessity.

Children must be educated from a wider perspective, taking into account the whole range of community activities. Schools ought to be kept open, much as libraries are, to serve as resources for community problem-solving, and after-school activities. The public schools are the only institutional establishment that can ensure an educated populace for the perpetuity of a democratic-republic society and serve as an opportunity for each individual to cultivate their best aspirations and dreams.

THE COMMUNITY AS A BULWARK AGAINST DELINQUENCY AND SOCIAL DISORDER

A s I mentioned at the beginning of this essay, the tribal instinct is in all of us, going to as far back as the Anthropologists have studied. This primitive instinct is what binds us into units, as small as the family and as large as nationhood. In recent times the world populace is seeing itself as a theatre of "globalization" which means that our concept of tribalization is, at least in an economical sense, becoming widespread internationally.

However, getting back to smaller details we must look at our communities and neighborhoods as a bulwark against delinquency and social disorder. In many areas of our nation, families and schools are not well secured and provide only marginal support for children growing up.

Great volunteer services are needed and are, indeed, available in most communities such as the Police Athletic League and Midnight Basketball.

CASA (Court Appointed Special Advocate) program and many volunteer services for youth are offered by churches and ancillary school activities. Anything that will help interface young people with local community resources and enlist their own services will inspire a young person to value himself or herself and that is important.

Also, there are volunteer services for young people to offer their skills and energy in such activities as: distributing goodwill clothing to those less fortunate along with toys and stuffed animals, sending off packages and cards to the military deployments, texting about political concerns to local representatives, collecting books for children who can't afford them as well as those who are hospitalized, helping to tutor those who are struggling with the language, raking leaves for the elderly, teaching computer skills to the elderly, taking people on tours of historic sites, volunteering to coach or referee at children's sports events, bake sales for charity and many more. The idea is to get young people interested in exploring their own inner resources, to enhance their sense of value and contribution. It's all about instilling young people with the feeling of being an important and useful member of the tribe.

Though there has been an insidious erosion of community trust and confidence in government and social processes in the past 40 or 50 years, those of the WWII era will often say that during the great World War, this nation pulled together and worked together as a united community with a common purpose of survival. That sense of communality and common purpose can and must be regained but without the conditions of war. That is the great challenge of the future and we can succeed if we want to. Most humans, it is largely agreed, desire a living environment that values a sense of cooperation and good will rather than mistrust and alienation, a sense of community built on a common noble purpose rather than social estrangement and isolation.

Maybe we have focused too much on the seductive powers of liberty and freedom and basic civil rights for individuals without attaching the true quality of those virtues to the concept of social responsibility. There may not be, in reality, a true quality of liberty, freedom, justice or rights without a sense of social responsibility and connectedness. Whether it be on an individual basis or on a societal basis or whether it be in the field of education, law, medicine, business, industry or politics, the society, as a whole, may be thwarted in its destined greatness, unless all of us espouse the traditional values of social integrity that this country was founded upon.

That is the crossing we all must make in order to feel re-connected to a noble national purpose and an ever-unfolding bright destiny.

The way people rallied around those who were so devastated by the Oklahoma City bombing of 1995 and the wonderful acts of courage and compassion that came from all parts of this country ought to serve as an inspiration. It goes to show that the American people still possess that indefatigable character and social integrity that served us well in all the great crises of the nation's history. In spite of all the indulgences of the past 50 years, we do live in a world of renewed hope. In the past 50 years, we all lived with the terrible possibility of global nuclear destruction.

The world has now seen the demise of the Communist Soviet Union and Russia is attempting to align itself with the Western world. There is international agreement that it is in everyone's interest to contain and control the proliferation of nuclear weapons. Those dreaded missiles are no longer the global threat as before except perhaps for a small number of renegade countries who might wish to endorse terrorism for their own interests, and even they can be dissuaded from evil intent. The United Nations is finding its role in the world and working toward maintaining a fragile peace in the tangled division of the world and specifically the Middle East. Continuing advances in medical technologies and pharmacology along with technical achievements and computerization have revolutionized life on this planet and promise a brighter future of greater need gratification for all peoples of the earth, thereby laying the groundwork for more effective cooperation and problem solving among the peoples of the earth.

Perhaps now, if we can responsibly address our problems at home, we may begin to look optimistically to the future with confidence to build and create rather than destroy, to enter an era of mutually assured cooperation rather than mutually assured destruction, to educate and train rather than indulge in projects of despair.

There now appears to be an emerging consciousness of the implications of social/ethical values in the workplace and the need to recognize the importance of human considerations in modern living. Some of the great corporations in the US are discovering that it is in their best interests to provide consideration for such human needs as flexi-time, in-house child care, maternity or paternity leave, counseling for those who must be reassigned or to have need for resolving personal crises, work-out facilities, and healthy lunch counters; coordinating with high schools in the process of matriculating young people into the labor market and assuring that they are suitably trained and directed and a generally more socially synergistic work environment. It is becoming more apparent that a need-gratified employee is a more productive employee, who can cope more effectively with the demands of the ever-increasing technologies.

The people's righteous anger is rising against the forces of impotence and negativity, and as has been the case in the past, when the American people are provoked to justifiable anger, the Ship of State will be reset on its true course while new technological systems and viable cultural values will assume a direction of purpose and thoughtful intention. There will be appeared changes in the wind. There is a new and exciting concept in education that does not yet have a full consensus of the American people, but it is growing in strength in various areas of the US It is characterized by an integration of the community and the school in a more dynamic and synergistic way. It stresses a melding of school and various community resources. It brings into focus the needs of educating children from a wider perspective, i.e. from the point of view of involved parents, educators, community policing and law, medical and mental health workers, and those in business and industry. Schools under the new system would be kept open as channels for learning, and community problem solving facilities, such as libraries, are kept open to the public as resource facilities and used for children's after school activities. Older, retired people would be brought into the schools as surrogate grandparents to offer emotional as well as educational support.

Promoting a revival of the American hope for the future and the re-vitalization of the society is by a whole-hearted support of three of society's most important institutions: the family, the public school and the community. In the final analysis, it is not a question of whether or not the public-school system can be saved. It must be saved otherwise the society will be dominated by an economic and educational elite. The public-school system is the only institution that assures a broad-based educated populace as this democratic republic requires, so that it may maintain and enhance itself in perpetuity. I say, let the focus for renewal first be placed upon the schools and the neighborhoods of those schools because that is where the hopes of parents can encourage their children in an upward direction. The public schools are where the minds, bodies and spirits of the children of America can be molded with strength and faith for the future. It is also the place in which real opportunity and independence can be fostered through the acquisition of life and workplace skills and self-understanding. Let us think, therefore, of hope for the future through opportunity in the public-school system as the key concept of American education. We only need give it a new vitality and enthusiasm. I believe the United States has a unique destiny to become a beacon of light to the world, but we are letting that precious beacon grow dim. Let us stand on the side of light rather than darkness. All this, I believe, will serve the interest of improving the criminal justice system in America and move in the direction of saving human resources rather than warehousing in a penal system that demonstrably does not work, and also, reducing violence and despair in America, as a way of life.

HOW IS THE BRAIN
IMPLICATED IN CHILD
DEVELOPMENT?

So, what determines the difference between a child that begins to become twisted into one that will grow up to become anti-social, or evil, as opposed to one that becomes socialized and one that is inspired to do good? To quote Daniel Goleman, Ph.D. in his book, "Social Intelligence," and referring to studies on the "peek-a-boo" game that mothers often play with their infants. If the mother is "attuned" to the emotional state of her child and allows the child to turn away, momentarily and take a time-out to suck its thumb, the child will shortly return for the excitement and pleasure of the game. If, however, the mother will not allow the child to take his felt need for a short respite but instead overpowers the child and forces its continued attention, this will begin a sense of threat to its need for approval and acceptance of its own needs. Goleman goes on to say, "Nothing can be proven by a single game of peek-a-boo. But repeated, multiple failures by a caretaker to attune, much research suggests, can have lasting effects. When reprised throughout childhood, these patterns shape the social brain in ways that make one child grow up delighted with the world, affectionate, and comfortable with people, while others grow up sad, and withdrawn, or angry and confrontational. Once, such differences might have been attributed to the child's temperament, a stand-in for genes. Now the scientific action centers on how a child's genes may be set by the thousands of routine interactions a child experiences growing up."

So, let us look more closely at how our brains work. Our brains develop with three major functions. The hind brain (reptilian so called) develops first in the mammalian species, which includes homo sapiens. This, we share with lower animals. It is composed of a spinal cord which sends sensory impulses up and down to various organs and peripheral nerves and muscles along with the medulla oblongata, the pons, and the cerebellum. This part of the brain controls such involuntary functioning, as basic as respiration, digestion, heart rate and blood circulation and functioning, sexual arousal, digestion, sneezing, and swallowing.

The second part of the brain to develop is the mid-brain or limbic system (the affective or emotional) which has to do with primary motivation or seeking such as wants and desires having to do with what satisfies and gives pleasure, contentment and wellbeing. This is called the parasympathetic system of the hypothalamus. There can also be a stimulus to another part of the hypothalamus that produces feelings of threat, unease and agitation, and this is called the sympathetic system. One type of stimulus produces feelings of peace and contentment and the other stimulus produces feelings of threat, hostility, and alarm as if one must to fight or run away from confrontation or simply freeze with terror. There is also another component of this system called the amygdala and hippocampus. The amygdala is the alarm signal and reacts to any sudden perception of threat. The hippocampus stores neural impulses for retention and learning. Such a signal will go to the sympathetic part of the hypothalamus and in turn trigger the pituitary gland and the adrenals for mobilization. In this case, adrenalin and cortisol are secreted into the blood stream causing physiological effects raising blood pressure, heart rate, respiration rate and other stress reactions that produce fear or anxiety. If a child's brain function becomes conditioned with too much sympathetic stimulation it will perceive its living environment as dangerous and threatening and react accordingly. In such a case instead of moving forward in its normal growth toward socialization it will tend toward an anti-social disposition. If some real threat is perceived such as a dangerous animal, we call that reaction fear. If the perception of threat is imagined, we call that anxiety.

Another part of the mid-brain is called the thalamus which transmits nerve signals such as sound, visual and somatic sensations.

The latest development of the brain in its evolution is the forebrain or neocortex, cognitive or thinking, which has to do with the executive or goal seeking capacity. It consists of a frontal lobe that commands and controls and is called the executive function because it evaluates, directs and plans for action to further one's goals. It also contains the parietal lobe which calculates movement and orientation. The temporal lobe is responsible for speech, sound, language and recognition. The occipital lobe controls visual sensation. Broca's area controls speech, language and facial nerves.

Finally, the corpus collosum bridges the two hemispheres of the brain and provides sensory integration. The two hemispheres account for linear-verbal intellection, left side, and spatial-performance intellection, right side, sometimes referred to as fluid intellection and crystalline intellection.

In child development, it is important to know that if a child is continually assaulted with threats, abuse and fears of abandonment, it will become so conditioned through the amygdala, the hippocampus and the sympathetic nervous system that the child, instead of moving forward with its normal developmental stages with confidence and self-assurance in pursuit of its emotional satisfactions, wants and desires will, instead, revert to a pre-occupation with its primary needs of security and compensation. Its emotional development will be arrested at an early stage and the child will grow immaturely and unable to distinguish its desires from its needs.

A SUMMARY STATEMENT ON CHILD DEVELOPMENT

Child development starts with the primary relationships in the family with a solid base of belonging, valuing and competence within a background of essential trust. In my view, it is essential for our society to enable mothers to be with their small children until they are well established in school. Someone once said that, "Children need roots and wings i.e. (emotional security and a sense of competence and then the freedom to explore the world of work and relationships)." It has also been said that, "The hand that rocks the cradle, rules the world" indicating how important it is for a child to have the attention and emotional support it needs from its most significant other.

Too many families are too highly stressed in today's American society and children are often neglected when they need the attention of their parents the most. Stress filters down to the children and creates anxiety and self-doubt. Too many young people are fearful and confused about the world they are about to inherit. An emotionally secure and tuned in mother and father can help their child along the way of their developmental tasks. So, they can experience basic trust, emerging autonomy, instead of self-doubt, initiative and competence, industry and assertiveness, instead of inferiority and identity, instead of confusion. By the time they emerge from adolescence they should have a firm grasp of themselves, who they are? a firm understanding of their interests and aptitudes, social disposition and the things they value.

All this self-knowledge ought to start in the home when a parent notices what objects and events seems to capture the child's interest and attention and what he/she seems to enjoy tampering with. As the child grows older, exploration should be encouraged, efforts and mistakes can be allowed with encouragement, within limits of safety of course, because a child must learn it is not a disgrace to fail at an honest attempt. In other words, encouragement works much better than scolding and criticism when it comes to helping a child develop a sense of self-competence and hence self-confidence.

I have always believed that one of the important roles of a school psychologist is to serve as an adjunct assistant to parents in how to best raise their children. As parents, we can all learn better ways to launch our children more effectively into adulthood. So, the school psychologist ought to be available for assistance and instruction. Evening classes can be arranged for that purpose or even private consultations. This, by the way, was an important responsibility of the juvenile probation officer, as I saw it, before new laws were enacted in the '60s that stressed legal issues rather than developmental ones.

As the child enters the school experience, a well-trained and perceptive teacher can further the child's development by continuing what the parents have begun, i.e. helping the child further discover the world of things and people in a productive way. Good teachers, for a child in those early formative years, are a treasure and ought to be rewarded as such. They set the tone and character for children in how they develop attitudes toward learning, responsible productivity and effective socialization.

The elementary grades ought to be an experience of further exploration both academically and in a community sense so that budding interests and aptitudes can be explored by each student as well as the concept of what it means to be a member of a community. I believe this is being done in some areas but sadly neglected in others.

Another important consideration has to do with the deterioration of professionalism among teachers. Teachers no longer dress like professionals, only administrators do, and that, in my opinion, not only marks the decline in teacher morale but signifies the public perception of teachers having an inferior status than administrators. It is the teacher that ought to be regarded as the true professional and ought to be financially rewarded as such.

In the high schools and community colleges, the schools, then, can support and encourage the continuation of this character development through exposure and guidance toward their inherited and learned propensities. The schools can provide the knowledge and skills necessary to develop the natural inclinations of the young person as well as the institutional foundations of the nation. Schools can encourage the matriculation into the adult world of work by providing realistic experiences in the community with actual time in a responsible tutorial or apprentice job. I started a program like this when I was the guidance counselor at an American school in Brazil. I placed seniors in various jobs according to their expressed interests for half a day, twice a week, and it proved very instructive for the students, and they appreciated the realistic introduction to what a job is all about.

Quality relationships can be studied so a young person understands the difference between a co-dependent and a healthy relationship before they choose a life-mate. There are tests that can and ought to be made available in the high schools, to those in need, that can greatly assist an unsure student as to abilities, interests, aptitudes, social disposition and uniqueness as to relating him or herself to the adult world of civil responsibilities. (To delve further into these matters read my book; How Goes it With America?)

As the child's brain development progresses, in the early stages, say around one and half years of age the mid-brain begins its maturation process, which will go on until the twenties, and the child will begin to assert itself as it strives for its own primitive self-hood. In other words, it begins to seek its own satisfactions and comforts. Some parents at this stage often experience what is perceived as a power struggle because the child wants to explore its surroundings and its own will to seek satisfaction. Parents of children reared in a strict Christian religious environment will often see this behavior as an indication of the child's essential self-serving evil or original sin. The child can be threatened with physical abuse or even threats of hell if he/she is perceived to be disobedient. The thwarting of an inherent and natural development often leads to rebellion, resentment and disturbing conflicts between the parent and the child or complete submission. If the child experiences enough threat to its survival, it will bid for abrogating its mandate for self-hood and capitulate to the parent's imposition of their needs and expectations. In such an unfortunate train of events the child will grow with pathological immaturity, lack of self-confidence and self-direction. Instead of following its wants and desires, it will follow its needs for approval, acceptance, and basic security. The child will not grow with a full sense of self-awareness and competence in following its own wants and desires. Rather, it will adopt what it has been taught by the authority of the parent or the church. To put it in other terms, the child at this early stage of development seeks a sense of pleasure and comfort and curiosity about himself and the world around him. The mid-brain functions, mentioned above, facilitate this. However, on the other hand if the normal developmental activity of the child experiences threat, the mid-brain will learn traits of anxious attachment to the parent, inhibition, self-doubt and confusion as to he/she really is. Abraham Maslow describes this as the "Psycho-pathogenesis of threat." This concept has now moved beyond theory, to a well-established protocol of child development. This type of personality development usually results in a hostility which can be turned inward to foster self-defeatism, depression, helplessness and hopelessness, or the hostility will be turned outward toward others as in a pathological anti-socialization.

Successful maturity, therefore, is the freedom to explore its wants and desires, within a safe environment, while immaturity is the result of too much prohibition of natural mid-brain development with resultant pre-occupation with need for security, approval, and acceptance, and escapes into fantasy or drugs. In such a case there are no sturdy roots in the character and therefore there can be no freedom to explore, desire and love with self-confidence. What makes it worse is that little children are often taught in a Christian home that they are basically evil, anyway, because of the sin of their original ancestors, Adam and Eve. Therefore, you must hang on desperately to the apron strings of "Mother Church" in order to be saved. In the Catholic faith, children are taught that, "Faith is a gift from God and, our response, is to believe in Him and we must, therefore, believe in Him in order to be saved and go to Heaven." This statement is from: "A Family of Faith" A Parent's Guide published, in 2017, by the Sophia Institute Press and by Mary Mosher, catechist, Founder of Holy Family Academy in Manchester, NH. The implication is that we cannot be saved unless we believe in Him and that, of course, is a gift of God, and if we cannot believe and be saved, the only alternative after death is hell. This book is taught for very young children at a local Catholic Church educational center in Northern California and, is purported to be standard fare for all Catholic educational facilities for children.

The Catholic Church, as an institution of religious learning, is only one of many denominations that teach dogmatic isms to their children, which stress the original evil nature of all of us and that suffering, and self-sacrifice is noble and good as well as fear, and guilt and shame as motivators for adhering to the way of salvation. This way of thinking, therefore, inadvertently contributes to the continual threats of disorder, violence and emotional disturbances in our world. Evil does not come from a devil, lurking around, trying to catch us in a time of weakness. Evil comes from us when we fail to provide the fresh water and earthly nutrients for our children in a safe and nurturing environment. People who ravage the earth and its people are not agents of Satan but are expressing their twisted motives in obtaining what they feel is their just deserves. The criminal thinking of individuals like that, is to say to themselves, "If I can't have the good things of life then I'm going to take them anyway and I want to make sure others can't have those things either."

In these dangerous times in the world we had better be extra careful and dampen this type of attitude because it could bring us to terrible consequences and, perhaps, even result in total annihilation of all sapiens. The earth is our "Garden of Eden." Let's nurture it for the generations to come rather than squander it senselessly.

Finally, in closing, it is my unquestioned belief that the future of America has a bright, beautiful and purposeful destiny for its upcoming generations. It only needs to be seeded with the important values that every parent wishes to impart to their child along with the affinity and cooperative spirit of a mutually interested community and a quality and professionally staffed school system.

About the Author

Harry Gael Michaels is a retired school psychologist who first entered his career as a juvenile probation officer in the 1960s. His writing of this essay is the result of witnessing an escalation of violence over the years in the nation.

He is also the author of *How Goes It with America, Wings Over Normandy, The State of the Republic, Reflections on Institutional Catholic-ism, An Educational and Family Friendly Prospectus,* and *Coping With Life: A Study in Adaptation.*